FROM THE LIBRARY OF

# Thoughts
## *for*
# Young Men

CALVARY PRESS

# Thoughts
## *for*
# Young Men

# *J.C. Ryle*

Calvary Press Publishing
P.O. Box 805
Amityville, NY 11701
U.S.A.
1 (800) 789-8175 / calvarypress.com
ISBN  1-879737-18-3

Cover Design: Anthony Rotolo

Ryle, J. C.
    Thoughts for Young Men
Recommended Dewey Decimal Classification:
248.4
Suggested Subject Headings:
1. Christian Living—Men's Interest
2. Religion—Christian Growth—Sanctification
I. Title

Manufactured in the United States of America
    4  5  6  7  8  9  10      03  04  05  06

# *PREFACE*

I have often wished that I had come across the writings of J.C. Ryle when I was a teenager. For while his books appeal to all ages and stages of Christian experience, their straightforward biblical wisdom and deep pastoral concern make them especially helpful at the formative stages of life.

Bishop Ryle wrote about the Christian life in a way that combined a searching spiritual rigor with a wonderfully healthy balance. *Thoughts for Young Men* illustrates these qualities. It abounds in reliable counsel and says - with a rare combination of seriousness and graciousness - the very things we need to hear. Young men, for whom it was written, will find it invaluable; but all Christians, men or women, young or old, can read it with lasting benefit. It deserves to be widely read and circulated, and will do spiritual good to every reader.

Sinclair B. Ferguson
Professor of Systematic Theology
Westminster Theological Seminary
Philadelphia, PA. USA

# *CONTENTS*

# THOUGHTS FOR YOUNG MEN

## John Charles Ryle

I send forth this little book for the special benefit of young men. When the Apostle Paul wrote his Epistle to Titus about his duty as a minister, he mentioned young men as a group requiring peculiar attention. After speaking of older men and older women, and young women, he adds this pithy advice, "Likewise, exhort the young men to be sober-minded" (Titus 2:6). I am going to follow the Apostle's advice. I propose to offer a few words of timely and friendly exhortation to young men.

I am growing old myself, but there are few things I remember so well as the days of my youth. I have a most distinct recollection of the joys and the sorrows, the hopes and the fears, the temptations and the difficulties, the mistaken judgments and the misplaced affections, the errors and the aspirations, which surround and accompany a young man's life. If I can only say something to keep some young man in the right way, and preserve him from faults and sins which may damage his well-being both for time and eternity, I shall be very thankful.

There are four things which I propose to do: First, I will mention some *general reasons* why young men need exhorting. Second, I will notice some *special dangers* against which young men need to be warned. Third, I will give some *general counsels* which I will entreat young men to receive. Fourth, I will set down some *special rules of conduct* which I strongly advise young men to follow.

On each of these four points I have something to say, and I pray to God that what I say may do good to your soul, dear reader.

# 1

## *Reasons for Exhorting Young Men*

In the first place, What are the general reasons why young men particularly need exhortation? Let me seek to mention several of them in order.

**(1) For one thing, there is the painful fact that there are few young men anywhere who seem to have any genuine religion.** I speak without respect of persons; I say it of all. High or low, rich or poor, gentle or simple, learned or unlearned, in town or in country, it makes no difference. I tremble to observe how few young men are led by the Spirit, how few are in that narrow way which leads to life, how few are setting their affections upon things above, how few are taking up the cross, and following Christ. I say it with all sorrow, but I believe, as in God's sight, I am saying nothing more than the truth.

Young man, you are one of a large and most important group in the population of your country;

but where, and in what condition, is your never-dying soul? Sadly, whatever way we turn for an answer, the report will be one and the same!

Let us ask any faithful minister of the gospel, and note what he will tell us. How many unmarried young people can he calculate who come to the Lord's Supper? Who are the most negligent about using the means of grace,[1] the most irregular about Sunday services, the most difficult to draw to weekly studies and prayer-meetings, the most inattentive under preaching at all times? Which part of his congregation fills him with most anxiety? Who are the Reubens for whom he has the deepest "searchings of heart"? (see Judges 5:16). Who in his flock are the hardest to manage, who require the most frequent warnings and rebukes, who occasion in him the greatest fear for their souls, and seem most hopeless? Depend on it, his answer will always be, *the young men.*

Let us ask the parents in any church throughout your country, and see what they will generally say. Who in their families give them most pain and trouble? Who need the most watchfulness, and most often disturb and disappoint them? Who are the first to be led away from what is right, and the last to remember cautions and good advice? Who are the most difficult to keep in order and bounds? Who most frequently break out into open sin, disgrace the family name, make their friends unhappy, embitter the old age of their relatives, and bring down gray hairs with sorrow to the grave? Depend upon it, the answer will generally be, *the young men.*

Let us ask the judges and police officers, and note what they will reply. Who frequent the bars and taverns the most? Who are the greatest Sabbath-breakers? Who make up riotous mobs and rebellious meetings? Who are most often hauled in for drunkenness, for disturbances of the peace, fighting, stealing, assaults, and the like? Who fill the jails, and the penitentiaries? Who are the class which requires the most incessant watching and looking after? Depend on it, they will at once point to the same section, they will say, *the young men.*

Let us turn to the wealthy, and note the report we shall receive from them. In one family the sons are always wasting time, health, and money, in the selfish pursuit of pleasure. In another, the sons will follow no particular profession, but fritter away the most precious years of their life in doing nothing. In another, they take up a profession as a mere game, but pay no attention to its duties. In another, they are always forming wrong alliances, gambling, getting into debt, associating with bad companions, keeping their friends in a constant fever of anxiety.

Regretably, rank, and title, and wealth, and education, do not prevent these things! Anxious fathers, and heart-broken mothers, and sorrowing sisters, could tell sad tales about them, if the truth were known. Many a family, with everything this world can give, numbers among its relations some name that is never named, or only named with regret and shame, some son, some brother, some cousin, some nephew, who must have his own way, and is thus a grief to all who know him.

There is seldom a rich family which does not have some thorn in its side, some blot in its page of happiness, some constant source of pain and anxiety; and often, far too often, is not this the true cause, *the young men*?

What shall we say to these things? These are facts, plain facts which stare us in the face, facts which meet us on every side, facts which cannot be denied. How dreadful this is! How dreadful the thought, that every time I meet a young man, I meet one who is in all probability an enemy of God, traveling in the broad way which leads to destruction, unfit for heaven! Surely, with such facts before me, you will not wonder that I exhort you as I do. Indeed, you must admit that there is a rightful cause for my concern.

**(2) For another thing, death and judgment are facing young men, even as others, and they nearly all seem to forget it.** Young man, it is appointed unto you once to die (Heb. 9:27); and however strong and healthy you may be now, the day of your death is perhaps very near. I see sickness in young people as well as old. I bury youthful corpses as well as aged. I read the names of persons no older than you in every graveyard. I learn from books that, except for infancy and old age, more die between thirteen and twenty-three than at any other season of life.[2] And yet you live as if you were sure at present not to die at all.

Are you thinking you will attend to these things *tomorrow*?    Remember the words of wise King Solomon: "Do not boast about tomorrow, for you do not know what a day may bring forth" (Proverbs 27:1). "Serious things tomorrow," said a heathen, to one who warned him of coming danger; but his tomorrow never came. Tomorrow is the devil's day, but today is God's. Satan cares not how spiritual your intentions may be, and how holy your resolutions, so long as they are fixed for *tomorrow*. Oh, give no place to the devil in this matter! Tell him, "No: Satan! It shall be today: today!" All men do not live to be patriarchs, like Isaac and Jacob. Many children die before their fathers. David had to mourn the death of his two finest sons; Job lost all ten of his children in one day. Your fate may be like one of theirs, and when death summons, it will be vain to talk of tomorrow, you must go at once.

Are you thinking you will have a *convenient season* to consider these things some day in the future? So thought Felix and the Athenians to whom Paul preached; but it never came (see Acts 17:32-34; 24:24-27). Hell is paved with such fancy and foolish notions. Better make sure work while you can. Leave nothing unsettled that is eternal. Run no risk when your soul is at stake. Believe me, the salvation of a soul is no easy matter. All need a "great" salvation, whether young or old; all need to be born again, all need to be washed in Christ's blood, all need to be sanctified by the Spirit. Happy is that man who does not leave these things uncertain, but never rests till he has the witness of the Spirit within him, that he is a child of God.

Young man, your time is short. Your days are but a span long, a shadow, a vapor, a tale that is soon told. Your bodies are not brass. "Even the young men," says Isaiah, "shall utterly fall" (Isa. 40:30). Your health may be taken from you in a moment: it only takes a fall, a fever, an inflammation, a broken blood-vessel, and the worm would soon feed upon you. There is but a step between you and death. This night your soul might be required of you. You are fast going the way of all the earth, you will soon be gone. Your life is all uncertainty, your death and judgment are perfectly sure. You too must hear the Archangel's trumpet, and go forth to stand before the great white throne. You too must obey that summons, which Jerome[3] says was always ringing in his ears: "Arise, you dead, and come to judgment." "Surely I come quickly," is the language of the Judge Himself (Rev. 22:20). I cannot, dare not, will not let you alone.

Oh that you would lay to heart the words of the Preacher: "Rejoice, O young man, in your youth, and let your heart cheer you in the days of your youth; walk in the ways of your heart, and in the sight of your eyes; but know that for all these God will bring you into judgment" (Eccles. 11:9). Astonishing, that with such an appointment, any man can be careless and unconcerned! Surely none are so foolish as those who are content to live unprepared to die. Surely the unbelief of men is the most amazing thing in the world. Well may the clearest prophecy in the Bible begin with these words. "Who has believed our report?" (Isa. 53:1). Well may the Lord Jesus say, "When the Son of man comes, will He really find faith on the earth?" (Luke 18:8). Young man, I fear lest this be the report of you in the courts above: "He will not believe." I fear lest you be hurried out of the world, and awaken to find out, too late, that death and judgment are realities. I fear all this, and therefore I exhort you.

**(3) For another thing, what young men will be, in all probability depends upon what they are now, and yet they seem so easily to forget this.** Youth is the seed-time of full age, the molding season in the little space of human life, the turning-point in the history of man's mind.

By the shoot we judge of the tree, by the blossoms we judge of the fruit, by the spring we judge of the harvest, by the morning we judge of the day, and by the character of the young man, we may generally judge what he will be when he grows up.

Young man, do not be deceived. Do not think you can willfully serve your self and your pleasures in the beginning of life, and then go and serve God with ease at the end. Do not think you can live with Esau, and then die with Jacob. It is a mockery to deal with God and your soul in such a fashion. It is an awful mockery to suppose you can give the flower of your strength to the world and the devil, and then put off the King of kings with the scraps and leftovers of your hearts, the wreck and remnant of your powers. It is an awful mockery, and you may find to your horror that the thing, in fact, cannot be done.

I venture to say you are counting on a *late repentance*. You do not know what you are doing. You are reckoning without God. Repentance and faith are the gifts of God, and gifts that He often withholds, when they have been long offered in vain. I grant you that true repentance is never too late, but I warn you at the same time, late repentance is seldom true. I grant you, one penitent thief was converted in his last hours, that no man might despair; but I warn you, only one was converted, that no man might presume (see Luke 23:39-43). I grant you it is written, Jesus is "able to save to the uttermost those who come to God by Him" (Heb. 7:25). But I warn you, it is also written by the same Spirit, "Because I have called, and you refused, I also will laugh at your calamity; I will mock when your terror comes" (Pro. 1:24,26).

Believe me, you will find it no easy matter to turn to God just when you please. It is a true saying of good Archbishop Leighton[4]: "The way of sin is down hill; a man cannot stop whenever he wishes." Holy desires and serious convictions are not like the servants of the Centurion, ready to come and go at your desire; rather are they like the unicorn in Job, they will not obey your voice, nor attend at your bidding. It was said of Hannibal, a famous general of old, when he could have taken the city of Rome which he warred against, he *would not*, and finally when he would, he *could not*. Beware, lest the same kind of event happen to you in the matter of eternal life.

Why do I say all this? I say it because of *the force of habit*. I say it because experience tells me that people's hearts are seldom changed if they are not changed when young. Seldom indeed are men converted when they are old. Habits have long roots. Sin once allowed to nestle in your bosom, will not be turned out at your bidding. Custom becomes second nature, and its chains are threefold cords not easily broken. Well does the prophet declare, "Can the Ethiopian change his skin, or the leopard his spots? Then may you also do good, who are accustomed to do evil" (Jer. 13:23). Habits are like stones rolling down hill, the further they roll, the faster and more uncontrollable is their course. Habits, like trees, are strengthened by age. A boy may bend an oak, when it is a sapling, a hundred men cannot root it up, when it is a full-grown tree. A child can wade over the River Thames at its fountainhead, the largest ship in the world can float in it when it gets near the sea. So it is with habits: the older they are the stronger they grow, the longer they have held possession of the soul, the harder they will be to cast out. They grow with our growth, and strengthen with our strength. Habit is the nurse of sin. Every fresh act of sin lessens fear and remorse, hardens our hearts, blunts the edge of our conscience, and increases our evil inclination.

Young man, you may imagine I am laying too much stress on this point. If you have seen old men, as I have done, on the brink of the grave, without any feeling, seared, callous, dead, cold, hard as the nether millstone,[5] you would not think so. Believe me, you cannot stand still in the affairs of your souls. Habits of good or evil are daily strengthening in your hearts. Every day you are either getting nearer to God, or further off. Every year that you continue unrepentant and unconverted, the wall of division between you and heaven becomes higher and thicker, and the gulf to be crossed deeper and broader. Oh, I urge you, dread the hardening effect of constant lingering in sin! Now is the accepted time. See that your flight be not in the winter of your days. If you seek not the Lord when young, the strength of habit is such that you will probably never seek Him at all. It is this I fear, and therefore I exhort you.

**(4) For another thing, the devil uses special diligence to destroy the souls of young men, and**

**yet they seem not to know it.** Satan knows well that you will make up the next generation, and therefore he employs every craft quickly and early to make you his own. I would not have you ignorant of his devices.

You are those on whom he displays all his choicest temptations. He spreads his net with the most watchful carefulness, to entangle your hearts. He baits his traps with the sweetest morsels, to get you into his power. He displays his merchandise before your eyes with his utmost ingenuity, in order to make you buy his sugared poisons, and eat his accursed dainties. You are the grand object of his attack. May the Lord rebuke him, and deliver you out of his hands.

Young man, beware of being taken by his snares. He will try to throw dust in your eyes, and prevent you from seeing anything in its true colors. He would willingly make you think evil good, and good evil. He will paint, and mask, and dress up sin, in order to make you fall in love with it. He will deform, and misrepresent, and caricature true religion, in order to make you take a dislike to it. He will exalt the pleasures of wickedness, but he will hide from you the sting. He will lift up before your eyes the cross and its painfulness, but he will keep out of sight the eternal crown. He will promise you everything, as he did to Christ, if you will only serve him. He will even help you to wear a form of religion, if you will only neglect the power. He will tell you at the beginning of your lives, it is *too soon* to serve God, he will tell you at the end, it is *too late*. Oh, be not deceived !

How little you know of the danger you are in from this dreadful enemy; and it is this very ignorance which makes me afraid. You are like a blind man, walking in the midst of holes and pitfalls; you do not see the perils which are around you on every side.

Your enemy is *mighty*. He is called "The Prince of this world" (John 14:30). He opposed our Lord Jesus Christ all through His ministry. He tempted Adam and Eve to eat the forbidden fruit, and so brought sin and death into the world. He tempted even David, the man after God's own heart, and caused his latter days to be full of sorrow. He tempted even Peter, the chosen Apostle, and persuaded him to deny his Lord. Surely his intense hatred must not be ignored!

Your enemy is *restless*. He never sleeps. He is always going about as a roaring lion, seeking whom he may devour (1 Pet. 5:8). He is ever going to and fro in the earth, and walking up and down in it (Job 1:7; 2:2). You may be careless about your soul: he is not. He wants it to make it miserable, like himself, and will have it if he can. Surely his intense hatred must not be ignored!

And your enemy is *cunning*. For many thousands of years he has been reading one book, and that book is the heart of man. He ought to know it well, and he does know it; all its weakness, all its deceitfulness, all its folly. And he has a store of temptations, such as are most likely to do it harm. Never will you go to the place where he will not find you. Go into towns, he will be there. Go into a wilderness, he will be there also. Sit among drunkards and partygoers, and he will be there to help you. Listen to preaching, and he will be there to distract you. Surely such intense hatred must not be ignored!

Young man, this enemy is working hard for your destruction, however little you may think it. You are the prize for which he is especially contending. He foresees that you must either be a blessing or a curse in your day, and he is trying hard to gain an early entrance into your hearts, in order that you may help further his kingdom in the end. Well does he understand that to spoil the bud is the surest way to ruin the flower.

Oh that your eyes were opened, like those of Elisha's servant in Dothan (2 Kings 6:15-17)! Oh that you did but see what Satan is scheming against your peace! I must warn you, I must exhort you.

Whether you will hear or not, I cannot, dare not, leave you alone.

**(5) For another thing, young men need exhorting, because of the sorrow it will save them to begin serving God now.** Sin is the mother of all sorrow, and no sort of sin appears to give a man so much misery and pain as the sins of his youth. The foolish acts he did, the time he wasted, the mistakes he made, the bad company he kept, the harm he did himself, both body and soul, the chances of happiness he threw away, the opportunities for usefulness he neglected; all these are things that often embitter the conscience of an old man, throw a gloom on the evening of his days, and fill the latter hours of his life with self-reproach and shame.

Some men could tell you of the untimely *loss of health*, brought on by youthful sins. Disease racks their limbs with pain, and life is almost a weariness. Their muscular strength is so wasted, that a grasshopper seems a burden. Their eye has become prematurely dim, and their natural force abated. The sun of their health has gone down while it is yet day, and they mourn to see their flesh and body consumed (Eccl. 12:1f.). Believe me, this is a bitter cup to drink.

Others could give you sad accounts of the *consequences of idleness*. They threw away the golden opportunity for learning. They would not get wisdom at the time when their minds were most able to receive it, and their memories most ready to retain it. And now it is too late. They no longer have the leisure time to sit down and learn. They no longer have the same power, even if they had the leisure. Lost time can never be redeemed. This too is a bitter cup to drink.

Others could tell you of grievous *mistakes in judgment*, from which they suffer all their lives long. They would have their own way. They would not take advice. They formed some alliance which has been altogether destructive to their happiness. They chose a profession for which they were entirely unsuited. And they see it all now. But tragically their eyes are only open when the mistake cannot be retrieved. Oh, this is also a bitter cup to drink!

Young man, young man, I wish you did but know the comfort of a conscience not burdened with a long list of youthful sins. These are the wounds that pierce the spirit. This is the iron that enters into the soul. Be merciful to yourself. Seek the Lord early, and so you will be spared many a bitter tear.

This is the truth that Job seems to have felt. He says, "For You write bitter things against me, and make me inherit the iniquities of my youth" (Job 13:26). So also his friend Zophar, speaking of the wicked, says, "His bones are full of the sins of his youth, which shall lie down with him in the dust" (Job 20:11).

David also seems to have felt it. He says to the Lord, "Do not remember the sins of my youth, nor my transgressions" (Psalm 25:7).

Beza,[6] the great Swiss Reformer, felt it so strongly, that he named it in his will as a special mercy that he had been called out from the world, by the grace of God at the age of sixteen.

Go and ask believers now, and I think many of them will tell you much the same. "Oh that I could live my younger days over again!" he will most probably say. "Oh that I had spent the beginning of my life in a better fashion! Oh that I had not laid the foundation of evil habits so strongly in the springtime of my life!"[7]

Young man, I want to save you all this sorrow, if I can. Hell itself is truth known too late. Be wise in time. What youth sows, old age must reap. Give not the most precious season of your life to that which will not comfort you in your latter days. Sow to yourself rather in righteousness: break up your fallow ground, sow not among thorns.[8]

Sin may go easily from your hand, or run smoothly off your tongue now, but depend upon it, you and sin will meet again before too long, however little you may like it. Old wounds will often ache and give pain long after they are healed, and only a scar remains: so may you find it with your sins. The footprints of animals have been found on the surface of rocks that were once wet sand, thousands of years after the animal that made them has perished and passed away; so also it may be with your sins.

"Experience," says the proverb, "keeps a dear school, but fools will learn in no other." I want you to escape the misery of learning in that school. I want you to avoid the wretchedness that youthful sins are sure to produce. This is the last reason why I exhort you.

# 2

## *Dangers Facing Young Men*

In the second place, there are some special dangers against which young men need to be warned.

**(1) One special danger to young men is the sin of pride.** I know well that all souls are in fearful danger. Old or young, it matters not; all have a race to run, a battle to fight, a sinful heart to mortify, a world to overcome, a body to keep under control, a devil to resist; and we may well say, "Who is sufficient for these things?" But still every age and condition has its own peculiar snares and temptations, and it is good to know them. He that is forewarned is forearmed. If I can only persuade you to be on your guard against the dangers I am going to name, I am sure I shall do your souls an essential service.

Pride is the oldest sin in the world. Indeed, it was before the world. Satan and his angels fell by pride. They were not satisfied with their first estate. Thus pride stocked hell with its first inhabitants.

Pride cast Adam out of paradise. He was not content with the place God assigned him. He tried to raise himself, and fell. Thus sin, sorrow and death entered into this world by pride.

Pride sits in all our hearts by nature. We are born proud. Pride makes us rest satisfied with ourselves, thinking we are good enough as we are. It closes our ears against all advice, refuses the gospel of Christ and turns every one to his own way. But pride never reigns anywhere so powerfully as in the heart of a young man.

How common it is to see young men headstrong, high-minded, and impatient of counsel! How often they are rude and uncourteous to all who are around them, thinking they are not valued and honored as they deserve to be! How often they will not stop to listen to a hint from an older person! They think they know everything. They are full of conceit of their own wisdom. They regard elderly people, and especially their relatives, to be stupid, and dull, and slow. They imagine that they need no teaching or instruction themselves: they understand all things. It makes them almost angry to be spoken to. Like young horses, they cannot bear the least control. They must be independent, and have their own way. They seem to think, like those whom Job mentioned, "We are the people, and wisdom shall die with us" (Job 12:2). And this is all pride.

Such an one was Rehoboam, who despised the counsel of the old experienced men who stood before his father Solomon, and hearkened to the advice of the young men of his own generation. He lived to reap the consequences of his folly (see 1 Kings 12). Sadly, there are many like him.

Such an one was the prodigal son in the parable, who must have the portion of his inheritance now, and set out for himself. He could not submit to live quietly under his father's roof, but must go into a far country, and be his own master. Like the little child who will leave its mother's hand and walk alone, he soon smarted for his foolishness. He finally became wiser when he was forced to eat husks with the swine (Luke 15:11-19). But, sadly, there are many like him.

Young man, I beseech you earnestly, beware of pride. Two things are said to be very rare sights in the world, one is a young man humble, and the other is an old man content. I fear this saying is only too true.

Be not proud of your own abilities, your own strength, your own knowledge, your own appearance, your own cleverness. Be not proud of yourself, and your talents of any kind. It all comes from not knowing yourself and the world. The older you grow, and the more you see, the less reason you will find for being proud. Ignorance and inexperience are the pedestal of pride; once let the pedestal be removed, and pride will soon come tumbling down.

Remember how often Scripture sets before us the excellence of a humble spirit. How strongly we are warned "not to think of (ourselves) more highly than (we) ought to think!" (Rom. 12:3). How plainly we are told, "If anyone thinks that he knows anything, he knows nothing yet as he ought to know!" (1 Cor. 8:2). How strict is the command, "Put on humbleness of mind!" (Col. 3:12). And again, "Be clothed with humility" (1 Pet. 5:5). Sadly, this is a garment of which many seem not to have so much as a scrap.

Think of the great example our Lord Jesus Christ leaves us in this respect. He washed the feet of His disciples, saying, "You should do as I have done to you" (John 13:15). It is written, "Though He was rich, yet for your sakes He became poor" (2 Cor. 8:9). And again, "He made Himself of no reputation, taking the form of a bondservant, and coming in the likeness of men; and being found in appearance as a man, He humbled Himself" (Phil. 2:7,8). Surely to be proud is to be more like the devil and fallen Adam, than like Christ. Surely it can never be ignoble and dishonoring to be like Him.

Think of the wisest man that ever lived; I mean, of course, Solomon. See how he speaks of himself as a "little child," as one who "knew not how to go out or come in,"or manage for himself (1 Kings 3:7,8). That was a very different spirit from his brother Absalom's, who thought himself equal to anything: "Oh that I were made judge in the land, and everyone who has any suit or cause would come to me, then I would give him justice" (2 Sam. 15:4). That was a very different spirit from his brother Adonijah's, who "exalted himself, saying, 'I will be king' " (1 Kings 1:5). Humility was the beginning of Solomon's wisdom. He writes it down as his own experience, "Do you see a man wise in his own eyes? There is more hope for a fool than for him" (Pro. 26:12).

Young man, lay to heart these Scriptures just quoted. Do not be too confident in your own judgment. Cease to be sure that you are always right, and others always wrong. Be distrustful of your own opinion, when you find it contrary to that of older men than yourself, and especially to that of your own parents. Age gives experience, and therefore deserves respect. It is a mark of Elihu's wisdom, in the book of Job, that "he waited till Job had spoken, because they were older than himself" (Job 32:4). And afterwards he said, "I am young in years, and you are very old; therefore I was afraid, and dared not declare my opinion to you. I said, 'Age should speak, and multitude of years should teach wisdom' " (Job 32:6,7). Modesty and silence are beautiful graces in young people. Never be ashamed of being a learner: Jesus was one at twelve years of age; when He was found in the temple, He was "sitting in the midst of the teachers, both listening to them, and asking them questions" (Luke 2:46). The wisest men would tell you they are always learners, and are humbled to find after all how little they really know. The great Sir Isaac Newton[9] used to say that he felt himself no better than a little child, who had picked up a few precious stones on the shore of the sea of knowledge.

Young man, if you would be wise, if you would be happy, remember this warning I give, *Beware of pride.*

**(2) Another danger to young men is the love of pleasure.** Youth is the time when our passions are the strongest, - and like unruly children, cry most loudly for indulgence. Youth is the time when we have generally most health and strength: death seems far away, and to enjoy ourselves in this life seems everything. Youth is the time when most people have few earthly cares or anxieties to take up their attention. And all these things help to make young men think of nothing so much as pleasure. "I serve lusts and pleasures:" that is the true answer many a young man should give, if asked, "Whose servant are you?"

Young man, time would fail me if I were to tell you all the fruits this love of pleasure produces, and all the ways in which it may do you harm. Why should I speak of partying, feasting, drinking, gambling, theatergoing, dancing, and the like? Few are to be found who do not know something of these things by bitter experience. And these are only examples. All things that give a feeling of excitement for the moment, - all things that drown thought, and keep the mind in a constant whirl, - all things that please the senses and gratify the flesh; - these are the sort of things that have mighty power at your time of life, and they owe their power to the love of pleasure. Be on your guard. Be not like those of whom Paul speaks, "Lovers of pleasure more than lovers of God" (2 Tim. 3:4).

Remember what I say: if you would cleave to earthly pleasures, - these are the things which *murder souls*. There is no surer way to get a seared conscience and a hard impenitent heart, than to give way to the desires of the flesh and mind. It seems to be nothing at first, but its impact is in the long run.

Consider what Peter says: "Abstain from fleshly lusts, which war against the soul" (1 Pet. 2:11). They destroy the soul's peace, break down its strength, lead it into hard captivity, make it a slave.

Consider what Paul says: "Put to death your members which are on the earth" (Col. 3:5). "Those who are Christ's have crucified the flesh, with its passions and lusts" (Gal. 5:24). "But I discipline my body, and bring it into subjection" (1 Cor. 9:27). Once the body was a perfect mansion of the soul; - now it is all corrupt and disordered, and needs constant watching. It is a burden to the soul, - not a helpmeet; a hindrance, - not an assistance. It may become a useful servant, but it is always a bad master.

Consider, again, the words of Paul: "But put on the Lord Jesus Christ, and make no provision for the flesh, to fulfill its lusts" (Rom. 13:14). "These," says Leighton, "are the words, the very reading of which so wrought with Augustine, that from a vile and immoral young man he turned and became a faithful servant of Jesus Christ."[10] Young man, I wish this might be the case with you.

Remember, again, if you will cleave to earthly pleasures, they are all *unsatisfying, empty and vain*. Like the locusts of the vision in Revelation, they seem to have crowns on their heads: but like the same locusts, you will find they have stings, - real stings, - in their tails. All is not gold that glitters. All is not good that tastes sweet. All is not real pleasure that pleases for a time.

Go and take your fill of earthly pleasures if you will, - you will never find your heart satisfied with them. There will always be a voice within, crying, like the horse-leech in Proverbs 30:15, "Give, give!" There is an empty place there, which nothing but God can fill. You will find, as Solomon did by experience, that earthly pleasures are but a vain show, - vanity and vexation of spirit, - whited sepulchers, fair to look at on the outside, full of ashes and corruption within. Better be wise in time. Better write "poison" on all earthly pleasures. The most lawful of them must be used with moderation. All of them are soul-destroying if you give them your heart.

And here I will not shrink from warning you and all young men to remember the seventh commandment; to beware of adultery and fornication, of all impurity of every kind. I fear there is often a lack of plain speaking on this part of God's law. But when I see how prophets and Apostles have dealt with this subject, - when I observe the open way in which the Reformers of our own Church denounce it, - when I see the number of young men who walk in the footsteps of Reuben, and Hophni, and

Phinehas, and Amnon, - I for one cannot, with a good conscience, hold my peace. I doubt whether the world is any better for the excessive silence which prevails upon this commandment. For my own part, I feel it would be false and unscriptural delicacy, in addressing young men, not to speak of that which is preeminently "*the young man's sin.*"

The breach of the seventh commandment is the sin above all others, that, as Hosea says, "takes away the heart" (Hos. 4:11). It is the sin that leaves deeper scars upon the soul than any sin that a man can commit. It is a sin that slays its thousands in every age, and has overthrown not a few of the saints of God in time past. Lot, and Samson, and David are fearful proofs. It is the sin that man dares to smile at, and smoothes over under the names of *entertainment, weakness* and *wildness.* But it is the sin that the devil peculiarly rejoices over, for he is the "unclean spirit;" and it is the sin that God peculiarly abhors, and declares He "will judge" (Hebrews 13:4).

Young man, I urge you, "flee sexual immorality" (1 Cor. 6:18) if you love life. "Let no one deceive you with empty words, for because of these things the wrath of God comes upon the sons of disobedience" (Eph. 5:6). Flee the *occasions* of it, - the company of those who might draw you into it, - the places where you might be tempted to it. Read what our Lord says about it in Matthew 5:28. Be like holy Job: "Make a covenant with your eyes" (Job 31:1). Flee *talking* of it. It is one of the things that ought not so much as to be named. You cannot handle tar and not be defiled. Flee the *thoughts* of it; resist them, mortify them, pray against them, - make any sacrifice rather than give way. Imagination is the hotbed where this sin is too often hatched. Guard your thoughts, and there is little fear about your deeds.

Consider the caution I have been giving. If you forget all else, do not let this be forgotten.

**(3) Another real danger to young men is thoughtlessness and lack of consideration.** Lack of thought is one simple reason why thousands of souls are cast away forever. Men will not consider, - will not look forward,- will not look around them,- will not reflect on the end of their present course, and the sure consequences of their present ways,- and awake at last to find they are damned for lack of thinking.

Young man, none are in more danger of this than you are. You know little of the perils around you, and so you are heedless how you walk. You hate the trouble of sober, quiet thinking, and so you form wrong decisions and run your heads into sorrow. Young Esau must have his brother's pottage and sell his birthright: he never *thought* how much he should one day want it (Gen. 25:27-34). Young Simeon and Levi must avenge their sister Dinah, and slay the Shechemites: they never *considered* how much trouble and anxiety they might bring on their father Jacob and his house (Gen. 34). Job seems to have been specially afraid of this thoughtlessness among his children: it is written, that when they had a feast, and "the days of their feasting were gone about, Job sent and sanctified them, and rose up early in the morning and offered burnt-offerings, according to the number of them all: for Job said, It may be that my sons have sinned, and cursed God in their hearts. Thus did Job continually" (Job 1:5).

Believe me, this world is not a world in which we can do well without thinking, and least of all do well in the matter of our souls. "Don't think," whispers Satan: he knows that an unconverted heart is like a dishonest businessman's books, it will not bear close inspection. "Consider your ways," says the Word of God, - stop and think, - consider and be wise. Well says the Spanish proverb, "Hurry comes from the devil." Just as men marry in haste and then repent at leisure, so they make mistakes about their souls in a minute, and then suffer for it for years. Just as a bad servant does wrong, and then says, "I never gave it a thought," so young men run into sin, and then say, "I did not think about it, - it did not look like sin." Not look like sin! What would you expect? Sin will not come to you, saying, "I am sin;" it would do little harm if it did. Sin always seems "good, and pleasant, and desirable," at the time of commission. Oh, get wisdom, get discretion! Remember the words of Solomon: "Ponder the path of your feet, and let all your ways be established" (Pro. 4:26). It is a wise saying of Lord Bacon,[11] "Do nothing rashly. Wait a little, that you make an end the sooner."

Some, I dare say, will object that I am asking what is unreasonable; that youth is not the time of life when people ought to be serious and thoughtful. I answer, there is little danger of their being too much so in the present day. Foolish talking, and jesting, and joking, and excessive merriment, are only too common. Doubtless there is a time for all things; but to be always light and trifling is anything but wise. What says the wisest of men? " It is better to go to the house of mourning than to go to the house of feasting: for that is the end of all men; and the living will lay it to heart. Sorrow is better than laughter: for by the sadness of the countenance the heart is made better. The heart of the wise is in the house of mourning; but the heart of fools is in the house of mirth" (Ecclesiastes 7:2-4). Matthew Henry[12] tells a story of a great statesman in Queen Elizabeth's time, who retired from public life in his latter days, and gave himself up to serious thought. His former lively companions came to visit him, and told him he was becoming melancholy: "No," he replied, "I am *serious*; for all are serious round about me. God is serious in observing us, - Christ is serious in interceding for us, - the Spirit is serious in striving with us, - the truths of God are serious, - our spiritual enemies are serious in their endeavors to ruin us, - poor lost sinners are serious in hell; - and why then should not you and I be serious too?"[13]

Oh, young man, learn to be thoughtful! Learn to consider what you are doing, and where you are going. Make time for calm reflection. Commune with your own heart, and be still. Remember my caution: - Do not be lost merely for the lack of thought.

**(4) Another danger to young men is a scornful contempt of religion.** This also is one of your special dangers. I always observe that none pay so little outward respect to religion as young men. None attend so poorly on means of grace, - none take so little part in our services, when they are present at them, - use Bibles and Prayer Books so little, - sing so little, - listen to preaching so little. None are so generally absent at prayer meetings, and Bible studies, and all such weekday helps to the soul. Young men seem to think they do not need these things, - they may be good for women and old men, but not for them. They appear ashamed of seeming to care about their souls: one would almost think they reckoned it a disgrace to go to heaven at all. And this is *contempt of religion*; it is the same spirit which caused the young people of Bethel to mock the godly Elisha (2 Kings 2:23); and of this spirit I say to you young man, Beware! If it is worthwhile to have a religion, it is worthwhile to be in earnest about it.

Contempt of holy things is the high road to infidelity. Once let a man begin to make a jest and joke of any part of Christianity, and I am never surprised to hear that he has turned out a downright unbeliever.

Young man, have you really made up your minds to this? Have you squarely looked into the gulf which stands before you, if you persist in despising religion? Call to mind the words of David: "The fool has said in his heart, There is no God" (Ps. 14:1). The *fool*, and none but the fool! - He has *said* it: but he has never proved it! Remember, if ever there was a book which has been proved true from beginning to end, by every kind of evidence, that book is the Bible. It has defied the attacks of all enemies and fault-finders. "The Word of the Lord is indeed *tried*"

(Psalm 18:30). It has been tried in every way, and the more it has been tried, the more evidently has it been shown to be the very handiwork of God Himself. What will you believe, if you do not believe the Bible? There is no choice but to believe something ridiculous and absurd. Depend on it, no man is so grossly credulous[14] as the man who denies the Bible to be the Word of God;[15] - and if it be the Word of God, take heed that you despise it not.

Men may tell you there are difficulties in the Bible; things hard to be understood. It would not be God's book if there were not. And what if there are? You do not despise medicines because you cannot explain all that your doctor does by them. But whatever men may say, the things needful to salvation are as clear as daylight. Be very sure of this, - people never reject the Bible because they cannot understand it. They understand it only too well; they understand that it condemns their own behavior; they understand that it witnesses against their own sins, and summons them to judgment. They try to believe it is false and useless, because they do not like to admit it is true. "A bad life," said the celebrated Lord Rochester,[16] laying his hand on the Bible, "a bad life is the only grand objection to this book." "Men question the truth of Christianity," says South[17], "because they hate the practice of it."

Young man, when did God ever fail to keep His word? Never. What He has said, He has always done; and what He has spoken, He has always made good. Did He fail to keep His word at the flood! - No. Did He fail with Sodom and Gomorrah? - No. Did He fail with Unbelieving Jerusalem? - No. Has He failed with the Jews up to this very hour? - No. He has never failed to fulfill His Word. Take care, lest you be found among those by whom God's Word is despised.

Never laugh at religion. Never make a jest of sacred things. Never mock those who are serious and in earnest about their souls. The time may come when you will count those happy whom you laughed at, a time when your laughter will be turned into sorrow, and your mockery into heaviness.

**(5) Another danger to young men is the fear of other's opinions**. "The fear of man" does indeed "bring a snare" (Pro. 29:25). It is terrible to observe the power which it has over most minds, and especially over the minds of the young. Few seem to have any opinions of their own, or to think for themselves. Like dead fish, they go with the stream and tide: what others think right, they think right; and what others call wrong, they call wrong too. There are not many original thinkers in the world. Most men are like sheep, they follow a leader.

If it was the fashion of the day to be Roman Catholics, they would be Roman Catholics, - if to be Islamic, they would be Islamic. They dread the idea of going against the current of the times. In a word, the opinion of the day becomes their religion, their creed, their Bible, and their God.

The thought, "What will my friends say or think of me? " nips many a good inclination in the bud. The fear of being looked upon, laughed at, ridiculed, prevents many a good habit from being taken up. There are Bibles that would be read this very day, if the owners dared. They know they ought to read them, but they are afraid: "What will people say?" There are knees that would be bent in prayer this very night, but the fear of man forbids it: "What would my wife, my brother, my friend, my companion say, if they saw me praying?" Oh, what wretched slavery this is, and yet how common! "I feared the people," said Saul to Samuel: and so he transgressed the commandment of the Lord (1 Sam. 15:24). "I am afraid of the Jews," said Zedekiah, the graceless king of Judah: and so he disobeyed the advice which Jeremiah gave him (Jer. 38:19). Herod was afraid of what his guests would think of him: so he did that which made him "exceedingly sorry," - he beheaded John the Baptist (Mark 6:17-28) . Pilate feared offending the Jews: so he did that which he knew in his conscience was unjust, - he delivered up Jesus to be crucified. If this is not slavery, tell me, what is?

Young man, I want you to be free from this bondage. I want you to care nothing for man's opinion, when the path of duty is clear. Believe me, it is a great thing to be able to say "No!" Here was good King Jehoshaphat's weak point, - he was too easy and soft in his dealings with Ahab, and thus came many of his troubles (1 Kings 22:4). Learn to say "No!" Let not the fear of seeming ill-natured make you unable to resist. When sinners entice you, be able to say decidedly, "I will not consent" (Pro. 1:10).

Consider how *unreasonable* this fear of man is. How short-lived is man's enmity, and how little harm he can do you! "Who are you, that you should be afraid of a man who will die, and of the son of a man who will be made like grass? And you forget the Lord your Maker, who stretched out the heavens, and laid the foundations of the earth?" (Isa. 51:12, 13). And how *thankless* is this fear! None will really think better of you for it. The world always respects those most who act boldly for God. Oh, break these bonds, and cast these chains from you! Never be ashamed of letting men see that you want to go to heaven. Think it no disgrace to show yourself to be a servant of God. Never be afraid of doing what is right.

Remember the words of the Lord Jesus: "Do not fear those who kill the body, but cannot kill the soul. But rather fear Him who is able to destroy both soul and body in hell" (Matthew 10:28). Only try to please God, and He can soon make others pleased with you. "When a man's ways please the Lord, He makes even his enemies to be at peace with him" (Pro. 16:7).

Young man, be of good courage.[18] Care not for what the world says or thinks: you will not be with the world always. Can man save your soul? No. Will man be your judge in the great and dreadful day of account? No. Can man give you a good conscience in life, a good hope in death, a good answer in the morning of resurrection? No! no! no! Man can do nothing of the sort. Then "fear not the reproach of men, neither be afraid of their revilings: for the moth shall eat them up like a garment, and the worm shall eat them like wool" (Isa. 51:7,8). Call to your mind the saying of good Colonel Gardiner:[19] "I fear God, and therefore I have none else to fear." Go and be like him.

Such are the warnings I give you. Lay them to heart. They are worth thinking over. I am much mistaken if they are not greatly needed. The Lord grant they may not have been given you in vain.

# 3

## *General Counsels to Young Men*

In the third place, I wish to give some general counsels to young men.

**(1) For one thing, try to get a clear view of the evil of sin.** Young man, if you only knew what sin is, and what sin has done, you would not think it strange that I exhort you as I do. You do not see it in its true colors. Your eyes are naturally blind to its guilt and danger, and therefore you cannot understand what makes me so anxious about you. Oh, let not the devil succeed in persuading you that sin is but a small, insignificant matter!

Think for a moment *what the Bible says about sin;* - how it dwells naturally in the heart of every man and woman alive (Eccles. 7:20; Rom. 3:23), - how it defiles our thoughts, words, and actions, continually (Gen. 6:5; Matt. 15:19), - how it renders us all guilty and abominable in the sight of a holy God

(Isa. 64:6; Hab. 1:13), - how it leaves us utterly without hope of salvation, if we look to ourselves (Ps. 143:2; Rom. 3:20), - how its fruit in this world is shame, and its wages in the world to come, death (Rom. 6:21,23). Think calmly of all this. I tell you this day, it is not more sad to be dying of cancer, and not to know it, than it is to be a living man, and not to know this.

Think *what an awful change sin has worked* on all our natures. Man is no longer what he was when God formed him out of the dust of the ground. He came out of God's hand upright and sinless (Eccles. 7:29). In the day of his creation he was, like everything else, "very good" (Gen. 1:31). And what is man now? - A fallen creature, a ruin, a being that shows the marks of corruption all over, - his heart like Nebuchadnezzar (Dan. 4), degraded and earthly, looking down and not up, - his *affections* like a household in disorder, calling no man master, all extravagance and confusion, - his *understanding* like a lamp flickering in the socket, impotent to guide him, not knowing good from evil, - his *will* like a rudderless ship, tossed to and fro by every desire, and consistent only in choosing any way rather than God's. Alas, what a wreck is man, compared to what he might have been! Well may we understand such figures being used as blindness, deafness, disease, sleep, death, when the Spirit has to give us a picture of man as he is. And man as he is, remember, was made so by sin.

Think, too, *what it has cost to make atonement for sin*, and to provide a pardon and forgiveness for sinners. God's own Son must come into the world, and take upon Him our nature, in order to pay the price of our redemption, and deliver us from the curse of a broken law. He who was in the beginning with the Father, and by whom all things were made, must suffer for sin the just for the unjust, - must die the death of a malefactor, before the way to heaven can be laid open to any soul. See the Lord Jesus Christ despised and rejected of men, scourged, mocked, and insulted; - behold Him bleeding on the cross of Calvary; - hear Him crying in agony, "My God, My God, why have You forsaken Me?" (Matt. 27:46) - mark how the sun was darkened, and the rocks torn apart at the sight; - and then consider, young man, what must be the evil and guilt of sin.

Think, also, *what sin has done* already upon the earth. Think how it cast Adam and Eve out of Eden, brought the flood upon the old world, caused fire to come down on Sodom and Gomorrah, drowned Pharaoh and his host in the Red Sea, destroyed the seven wicked nations of Canaan, scattered the twelve tribes of Israel over the face of the globe. Sin alone did all this.

Think, moreover, of all the *misery and sorrow that sin has caused*, and is causing at this very day. Pain, disease, and death, strifes, quarrels, and divisions, envy, jealousy, and malice, deceit, fraud, and cheating, violence, oppression, and robbery, selfishness, unkindness, and ingratitude; all these are the fruits of sin. Sin is the parent of them all. Indeed, it is sin that has so marred and spoiled the face of God's creation.

Young man, consider these things, and you will not wonder that we warn you as we do. Surely, if you did but think of them, you would break off with sin forever. Will you play with poison? Will you frolic with hell? Will you take fire in your hand? Will you harbor your deadliest enemy in your bosom? Will you go on living as if it did not matter at all whether your own sins were forgiven or not, - whether sin had dominion over you, or you over sin? Oh, awake to a sense of sin's sinfulness and danger! Remember the words of Solomon: "Fools," none but fools, "mock at sin" (Pro. 14:9).

Hear, then, the request that I make of you this day, - pray that God would teach you the real evil of sin. If you would have your soul saved, arise now and pray.

(2) **For another thing, seek to become acquainted with our Lord Jesus Christ.** This is, indeed, the principal thing in religion. This is the cornerstone of Christianity. Till you know this, my warnings and advice will be useless, and your endeavors, whatever they may be, will be in vain. A watch without a mainspring is not more unserviceable than is religion without Christ.

But let me not be misunderstood. It is not the mere knowing Christ's name that I mean, - it is the knowing His mercy, grace, and power, - the knowing Him not by the hearing of the ear, but by the experience of your heart. I want you to know Him by faith, - I want you, as Paul says, to know "the power of His resurrection; being conformed to His death" (Phil. 3:10). I want you to be able to say of Him, He is my peace and my strength, my life and my consolation, my Physician and my Shepherd, my Savior and my God.

Why do I make such a point of this? I do it because in Christ alone "all fullness dwells" (Col. 1:19), - because in Him alone there is full supply of all that we require for the necessities of our souls. Of ourselves we are all poor, empty creatures,

- empty of righteousness and peace, - empty of strength and comfort, - empty of courage and patience, - empty of power to stand, or go on, or make progress in this evil world. It is in Christ alone that all these things are to be found, - grace, peace, wisdom, righteousness, sanctification, and redemption. It is just in proportion as we live upon Him, that we are strong Christians. It is only when self is nothing and Christ is all our confidence, it is then only that we shall do great exploits (see Daniel 11:32). Then only are we armed for the battle of life, and shall overcome. Then only are we prepared for the journey of life, and shall get forward. To live on Christ, - to draw all from Christ, - to do all in the strength of Christ, - to be ever looking unto Christ; - this is the true secret of spiritual prosperity. "I can do all things," says Paul, "through Christ who strengthens me" (Phil. 4:13).

Young man, I set before you Jesus Christ this day, as the *treasury of your souls;* and I invite you to begin by going to Him, if you would so run as to obtain. Let this be your first step, - go to Christ. Do you want to consult friends? - He is the best friend: "a friend that sticks closer than a brother"- (Pro.18:24). Do you feel unworthy because of your sins? - Fear not: His blood cleanses from all sin. He says, "Though your sins are like scarlet, they shall be as white as snow: though they are red like crimson, they shall be as wool" (Isa. 1:18). Do you feel weak, and unable to follow Him? - Fear not: He will give you power to become sons of God. He will give you the Holy Spirit to dwell in you, and seal you for His own; a new heart will He give you, and a new spirit will He put within you. Are you troubled or beset with peculiar infirmities? Fear not: there is no evil spirit that Jesus cannot cast out, - there is no disease of soul that He cannot heal. Do you feel doubts and fears? Cast them aside: "Come unto Me," He says; "him that comes I will by no means cast out" (Jn. 6:37). He knows well the heart of a young man. He knows your trials and your temptations, your difficulties and your foes. In the days of His flesh He was like yourself, - a young man at Nazareth. He knows by experience a young man's mind. He can be touched with the feeling of your infirmities, - for He suffered Himself, being tempted. Surely you will be without excuse if you turn away from such a Savior and Friend as this.

Hear the request I make of you this day, - if you love life, seek to become acquainted with Jesus Christ.[20]

**(3) For another thing, never forget that nothing is so important as your soul.** Your soul is eternal. It will live forever. The world and all that it contains shall pass away, - firm, solid, beautiful, well-ordered as it is, the world shall come to an end. "The earth and the works that are in it shall be burned up" (2 Pet. 3:10). The works of statesmen, writers, painters, architects, are all short-lived: your soul will outlive them all. The angel's voice shall proclaim one day, that "Time shall be no longer" (Rev. 10:6). But that shall never be said of your souls.

Try, I beseech you, to realize the fact, that your soul is the one thing worth living for. It is the part of you which ought always to be first considered. No place, no employment is good for you, which injures your soul. No friend, no companion deserves your confidence, who makes light of your soul's concerns. The man who hurts your body, your property, your character, does you but temporary harm. He is the true enemy who seeks always to damage your soul.

Think for a moment. What were you sent into the world for? Not merely to eat and drink, and indulge the desires of the flesh, - not merely to dress up your body, and follow its lusts wherever they may lead you, - not merely to work, and sleep, and laugh, and talk, and enjoy yourself, and think of nothing but time. No! you were meant for something higher and better than this. You were placed here to train for eternity.[21] Your body was only intended to be a house for your never-dying spirit. It is flying in the face of God's purposes to do as many do, - to make the soul a servant to the body, and not the body a servant to the soul.

Young man, God is no respecter of persons. He regards no man's coat, or wallet, or rank, or position. He sees not with man's eyes (see 1 Samuel 16:7). The poorest saint that ever died in a workhouse is nobler in His sight than the richest sinner that ever died in a palace. God does not look at riches, titles, learning, beauty, or anything of the kind. One thing only God does look at, and that is the never-dying soul. He measures all men by one standard, one measure, one test, one criterion, and that is *the condition of their souls*.

Do not forget this. Keep in view, morning, noon, and night, the interests of your soul. Rise up each day desiring that it may prosper, - lie down each evening inquiring of yourself whether it has really made progress. Remember Zeuxis[22], the great painter of old. When men asked him why he labored so intensely, and took such extreme pains with every picture, his simple answer was, "I paint for eternity." Do not be ashamed to be like him. Set your never-dying soul before your mind's eye, and when men ask you why you live as you do, answer them in his spirit, "I live for my soul." Believe me, the day is fast approaching when the soul will be the one thing men will think of, and the only question of importance will be this, *"Is my soul lost or saved?"*

**(4) For another thing, remember that it is possible to be a young man and yet to serve God.** I fear the snares that Satan lays for you on this point. I fear lest he succeed in filling your minds with the vain notion, that to be a true Christian in youth is impossible. I have seen many carried away by this delusion. I have heard it said, "You are requiring impossibilities in expecting so much religion from young people. Youth is no time for seriousness. Our desires are strong, and it was never intended that we should keep them under control, as you wish us to do. God meant us to enjoy ourselves. There will be time enough for religion later on." And this kind of talk is only too much encouraged by the world. The world is only too ready to wink at youthful sins. The world appears to take it for granted that young men must "sow their wild oats." The world seems to take it for granted young people *must* be irreligious, and that it is not possible for them to follow Christ.

Young man, I will ask you this simple question, Where will you find anything of all this in the Word of God? Where is the chapter or verse in the Bible which will support this talking and reasoning of the world? Does not the Bible speak to old and young alike, without distinction? Is not sin, sin, whether committed at the age of twenty or fifty? Will it form the slightest excuse, in the Day of Judgment, to say, "I know I sinned, but then I was young"? Show your common sense, I beg of you, by giving up such vain excuses. You are responsible and accountable to God from the very moment that you know right and wrong.

I know well there are many difficulties in a young man's way, - I admit it fully. But there are always difficulties in the way of doing right. The path to heaven is always narrow, whether we be young or old (see Jesus' words in Matt. 7:13,14).

There are difficulties, - but God will give you grace to overcome them. God is no hard master. He will not, like Pharaoh, require you to make bricks without straw. He will make sure the path of plain duty is never impossible. He never laid commands on man which He will not give man power to perform.[23]

There are difficulties, - but many a young man has overcome them up to now, and so may you. *Moses* was a young man of like passions with yourself; but see what is said of him in Scripture: "By faith Moses, when he became of age, refused to be called the son of Pharaoh's daughter; choosing rather to suffer affliction with the people of God, than to enjoy the passing pleasures of sin; esteeming the reproach of Christ greater riches than the treasures in Egypt: for he looked to the reward" (Heb. 11:24-26). *Daniel* was a young man when he began to serve God in Babylon. He was surrounded by temptations of every kind. He had few with him, and many against him. Yet Daniel's life was so blameless and consistent, that even his enemies could find no fault in him, except "concerning the law of his God" (Dan. 6:5). And these are not solitary cases. There is a cloud of witnesses whom I could name. Time would fail me, if I were to tell you of young Isaac, young Joseph, young Joshua, young Samuel, young David, young Solomon, young Obadiah, young Josiah, young Timothy[24]. These were not angels, but men, with hearts naturally like your own. They too had obstacles to contend with, lusts to mortify, trials to endure, hard places to fill, just like yourself. But young as they were, they all found it possible to serve God. Will they not all rise in judgment and condemn you, if you persist in saying it cannot be done?

Young man, *try* to serve God. Resist the devil when he whispers it is impossible. Try, - and the Lord God of the promises will give you strength in the trying. He loves to meet those who struggle to come to Him, and He will meet you and give you the power that you feel you need. Be like the man whom

Bunyan's Pilgrim[25] saw in the Interpreter's house, - go forward boldly, saying, "Set down my name." Those words of our Lord are true, though I often hear them repeated by heartless and callous tongues: "Seek, and you will find; knock, and it will be opened to you" (Matt. 7:7). Difficulties which seemed like mountains shall melt away like snow in spring. Obstacles which seemed like giants in the hazy distance, shall dwindle into nothing when you squarely face them. The lion in the way which you fear, shall prove to be chained. If men believed the promises more, they would never be afraid of duties. But remember that little word I press upon you, and when Satan says, "You cannot be a Christian while you are young:" answer him, "Get behind me, Satan: by God's help *I will try*."

**(5) For another thing, determine as long as you live to make the Bible your guide and adviser.** The Bible is God's merciful provision for sinful man's soul, - the map by which he must steer his course, if he would attain eternal life. All that we need to know, in order to make us peaceful, holy, or happy, is there richly contained. If a young man wants to know how to begin life well, let him hear what David says: "How can a young man cleanse his way? By taking heed according to Your Word" (Ps. 119:9).[26]

Young man, I challenge you to make a habit of reading the Bible, and not to let the habit be broken. Let not the laughter of companions, - let not the bad customs of the family you may live in, - let none of these things prevent your doing it. Determine that you will not only *have* a Bible, but also make time to *read* it too.[27] Permit no man to persuade you that it is only a book for Sunday School children and old women. It is the book from which King David got wisdom and understanding. It is the book which young Timothy knew from his childhood. Never be ashamed of reading it. Do not "despise the Word" (Pro. 13:13).

Read it *with prayer* for the Spirit's grace to make you understand it. Bishop Beveridge[28] said, "A man may as soon read the letter of Scripture without eyes, as understand the spirit of it without grace."

Read it *reverently*, as the Word of God, not of man, - believing implicitly that what it approves is right, and what it condemns is wrong. Be very sure that every doctrine which will not stand the test of Scripture is false. This will keep you from being tossed to and fro, and carried about by the dangerous opinions of these latter days. Be very sure that every *practice* in your life which is contrary to Scripture, is sinful and must be given up. This will settle many a question of conscience, and cut the knot of many a doubt. Remember how differently two kings of Judah read the Word of God: Jehoiakim read it, and at once cut the writing to pieces, and burned it on the fire (Jer. 36:23). And why? - Because his heart rebelled against it, and he was resolved not to obey. Josiah read it, and at once rent his clothes, and cried mightily to the Lord (2 Chron. 34:19). And why? - Because his heart was tender and obedient. He was ready to do anything which Scripture showed him was his duty. Oh that you may follow the last of these two, and not the first!

And read it *regularly*. This is the only way to become "mighty in the Scriptures." A hasty glance at the Bible now and then does little good. At that rate you will never become familiar with its treasures, or feel the sword of the Spirit fitted to your hand in the hour of conflict. But get your mind stored with Scripture, by diligent reading, and you will soon discover its value and power. Texts will rise up in your hearts in the moment of temptation. Commands will suggest themselves in seasons of doubt. Promises will come across your thoughts in the time of discouragement. And thus you will experience the truth of David's words, "Your Word I have hidden in my heart, that I might not sin against You" (Ps. 119:11); and soundness of Solomon's words, "When you roam, they will lead you; when you sleep, they will keep you; and when you awake, they will speak with you" (Pro. 6:22).

I dwell on these things more because this is an age of reading.[29] Of making many books there seems no end, though few of them are really profitable. There seems a rage for cheap printing and publishing. Newspapers of every sort abound, and the tone of some, which have the widest circulation, speaks badly for the taste of the age. Amidst the flood of dangerous reading, I plead for my Master's book. I call upon you not to forget the book of the soul. Let not newspapers, novels and romances be read, while the prophets and Apostles lie despised. Let not the exciting and lustful swallow up your attention, while the edifying and the sanctifying can find no place in your mind.

Young man, give the Bible the honor due to it every day you live. Whatever you read, read that first. And beware of bad books: there are plenty in this day. Take heed what you read. I suspect there is more harm done to souls in this way than most people have an idea is possible. Value all books in proportion as they are agreeable to Scripture. Those that are nearest to it are the best, and those that are farthest from it, and most contrary to it, the worst.

**(6) And finally, one more thing, never make an intimate friend of anyone who is not a friend of God.** Understand me, I do not speak of *acquaintances*. I do not mean that you ought to have nothing to do with any but true Christians. To take such a position is neither possible nor desirable in this world. Christianity asks no man to be uncourteous.

But I do advise you to be very careful in your choice of *friends*. Do not open all your heart to a man merely because he is clever, agreeable, good-natured, high-spirited and kind. These things are all very well in their way, but they are not everything. Never be satisfied with the friendship of anyone who will not be useful to your soul.

Believe me, the importance of this advice cannot be overrated. There is no telling the harm that is done by associating with godless companions and friends. The devil has few better helps in ruining a man's soul. Grant him this help, and he cares little for all the armor with which you may be armed against him. Good education, early habits of morality, sermons, books, carefully regulated homes, letters of parents, all, he knows well, will avail you little, if you will only cling to ungodly friends. You may resist many open temptations, refuse many plain snares; but once take up with a bad companion, and he is content. That awful chapter which describes Amnon's wicked conduct about Tamar, almost begins with these words, "But Amnon had a friend, a very crafty man" (2 Samuel 13:3).

You must remember, we are all creatures of imitation: precept may teach us, but it is example that draws us. There is something in us all, that we are always disposed to catch the ways of those with whom we live; and the more we like them, the stronger does the disposition grow. Without our being aware of it, they influence our tastes and opinions. We gradually give up what they dislike, and take up what they like, in order to become closer friends with them. And worst of all we catch their ways in things that are wrong, far quicker than in things that are right. Health, unhappily, is not contagious, but disease is. It is far more easy to catch a chill than to impart a glow, and to make each other's religion dwindle away, than grow and prosper.

Young man, I ask you to lay these things to heart. Before you let any one become your constant companion, before you get into the habit of telling him everything, and going to him in all your troubles and all your pleasures, - before you do this, just think of what I have been saying; ask yourself, "Will this be a useful friendship to me or not?"

"Evil company" does indeed "corrupt good habits" (1 Cor. 15:33). I wish that text were written in hearts as often as it is in notebooks. Good friends are among our greatest blessings; - they may keep us back from much evil, quicken us in our course, speak a word in season, draw us upward, and draw us on. But a bad friend is a positive misfortune, a weight continually dragging us down, and chaining us to earth. Keep company with an irreligious man, and it is more than probable you will in the end become like him. That is the general consequence of all such friendships. The good go down to the bad, and the bad do not come up to the good. Even a stone will give way before the continual dripping of water. The world's proverb is only too correct: "Clothes and company tell true tales about one's character." "Show me who a man lives with," says the Spaniards, "and I will show you what he is."

I dwell more upon this point, because it has more to do with your well-being in life than at first sight appears. If ever you marry, it is more than probable you will choose a wife among the connections of your friends. If Jehoshaphat's son Jehoram had not formed a friendship with Ahab's family, he would most likely not have married Ahab's daughter. And who can estimate the importance of a right choice in marriage? It is a step which, according to the old saying, "either makes a man or mars him." Your happiness in both lives may depend on it. Your wife must either help your soul or harm it: there is no neutral. She will either fan the flame of religion in your heart, or throw cold water upon it, and make it burn low. She will either be wings or fetters, a rein or a spur to your Christianity, according to her character. He that finds a good wife does indeed "find a good thing;" but if you have the least wish to find one, be very careful how you choose your friends.

Do you ask me what kind of friends you shall choose? Choose friends who will benefit your soul, friends whom you can really respect, friends whom you would like to have near you on your deathbed, friends who love the Bible, and are not afraid to speak to you about it, friends such as you will not be ashamed of acknowledging at the coming of Christ, and the Day of Judgment. Follow the example that David sets for you when he says, "I am a companion of all who fear You, and of those who keep Your precepts" (Psalm 119:63). Remember also the words of Solomon: "He who walks with wise men will be wise; but the companion of fools will be destroyed" (Pro. 13:20). But depend on it, bad company in the present life, is the sure way to obtain worse company in the life to come.

# 4

## *Special Rules for Young Men*

In the last place, I will set down some particular rules of conduct which I strongly advise all young men to follow.

**(1) For one thing, resolve at once, by God's help, to break off every known sin, however small.** Look within. Examine your own heart. Do you see there any habit or custom which you know to be wrong in the sight of God? If you do, do not delay a moment in attacking it. Resolve at once to lay it aside.

Nothing darkens the eyes of the mind so much, and deadens the conscience so surely, as *an allowed sin*. It may be a little one, but it is not the less dangerous for all that. A small leak will sink a great ship, and a small spark will kindle a great fire, and a little allowed sin in the same way will ruin a never-dying soul. Take my advice, and never spare a little sin. Israel was commanded to slay every Canaanite, both great and small. Act on the same principle, and show no mercy to little sins. Well says the wise man Solomon, "Take us the foxes, the *little* foxes, that spoil the vines" (Song of Solomon 2:15).

Be sure no wicked man ever meant to be so wicked at his first beginning. But he began with allowing himself some *little* transgression, and that led on to something greater, and that in time produced something greater still, and thus he became the miserable being that he now is. When Hazael heard from Elisha of the horrible acts that he would one day do, he said with astonishment, "But what is your servant - a dog, that he should do this gross thing?" (2 Kings 8:13). But he allowed sin to take root in his heart, and in the end he did them all.

Young man, resist sin in its beginning. They may look small and insignificant, but mind what I say, resist them, - make no compromise, let no sin lodge quietly and undisturbed in your heart. "The mother of mischief," says an old proverb, "is no bigger than a midge's wing."[30] There is nothing finer than the point of a needle, but when it has made a hole, it draws all the thread after it. Remember the Apostle's words, "A little leaven leavens the whole lump" (1 Cor. 5:6).

Many a young man could tell you with sorrow and shame, that he traces up the ruin of all his worldly well-being to the point I am speaking of, - to giving way to sin in its beginnings. He began with habits of falsehood and dishonesty in little matters, and they grew upon him. Step by step, he has gone on from bad to worse, till he has done things that at one time he would have thought impossible; till at last he has lost his place, lost his character, lost his comfort, and well-nigh lost his soul. He allowed a gap in the wall of his conscience, because it seemed a little one, - and once allowed, that gap grew larger every day, till at length the whole wall seemed to come down.

Remember this especially in matters of *truth* and *honesty*. Make conscience of the most seemingly insignificant matters. "He who is faithful in what is least, is faithful also in much" (Luke 16:10). Whatever the world may choose to say, there are no little sins. All great buildings are made up of little parts. The first stone is as important as any other. All habits are formed by a succession of little acts, and the first little act is of mighty consequence. The ax in the fable only begged the trees to let him have one little piece of wood to make a handle, and he would never trouble them any more. He got it, and then he soon cut them all down. The devil only wants to get the wedge of a little allowed sin into your heart, and you will soon be all his own. It is a wise saying of old William Bridge,[31] "There is nothing small between us and God, for God is an infinite God."

There are two ways of coming down from the top of a church steeple; one is to jump down, - and the other is to come down by the steps: but both will lead you to the bottom. So also there are two ways of going to hell; one is to walk into it with your eyes open, - few people do that; the other is to go down by the steps of little sins, - and that way, I fear, is only too common. Put up with a few little sins, and you will soon want a few more. Even a heathen[32] could say, "Whoever was content with only one sin?" And then your course will be regularly worse and worse every year. Well did Jeremy Taylor[33] describe the progress of sin in a man: "First it startles him, then it becomes pleasing, then easy, then delightful, then frequent, then habitual, then confirmed! then the man is impenitent, then obstinate, then resolves never to repent, and finally he is damned."

Young man, if you would not come to this tragic end, recall the rule I give you this day, and resolve at once to break off every known sin.

**(2) For another thing, resolve, by God's help, to shun everything which may prove an occasion**

**of sin.** It is an excellent saying of good Bishop Hall,[34] "He who would be safe from the acts of evil, must widely avoid the occasions of it."[35] It is not enough that we determine to commit no sin, we must carefully keep at a distance from all approaches to it. By this test we ought to try our ways of spending our time, - the books that we read, the families that we visit, the society into which we go. We must not content ourselves with saying, "There is nothing positively wrong here;" we must go further, and say, "Is there anything here which may prove to me the occasion of stumbling into sin?"

This, be it remembered, is one great reason why *idleness* is so much to be avoided. It is not that doing nothing is of itself so positively wicked; it is the opportunity it affords to evil thoughts, and vain imaginations; it is the wide door it opens for Satan to throw in the seeds of bad things; it is this which is mainly to be feared. If David had not given occasion to the devil, by idling away his time on his housetop at Jerusalem (2 Samuel 11:1f.), he would probably never have seen Bathsheba, nor murdered Uriah.

This, too, is one great reason why *worldly amusements* are so objectionable. It may be difficult, in some instances, to show that they are, in themselves, positively unscriptural and wrong. But there is little difficulty in showing that the *tendency* of almost all of them is most injurious to the soul. They sow the seeds of an earthly and sensual frame of mind. They war against the life of faith. They promote an unhealthy and unnatural craving after excitement. They minister to the lust of the flesh, and the lust of the eye, and the pride of life. They dim the view of heaven and eternity, and give a false color to the things of time. They make the heart unfit for private prayer, and Scripture reading, and calm communion with God. The man who mingles in them is like one who gives Satan vantage ground. He has a battle to fight, and he gives his enemy the help of sun, and wind, and hill. It would be strange indeed if he did not find himself continually overcome.

Young man, endeavor, as much as in you lies, to keep clear of everything which may prove injurious to your soul. Never hold a candle to the devil. People may say you are over scrupulous, too particular, where is the mighty harm of such and such things? But do not heed them. It is dangerous to play tricks with sharp-edged tools: it is far more dangerous to take liberties with your never-dying soul. He that would be safe must not come near the brink of danger. He must look upon his heart as a keg of gunpowder, and be cautious not to handle one spark of temptation more than he can help.

What is the use of your praying, "Lead us not into temptation," unless you are yourself careful not to run into it; and "deliver us from evil," unless you show a desire to keep out of its way? Take for example, Joseph; not only did he refuse the seductive advances of his master's wife, but he showed his prudence in refusing to be "with her" at all (Gen. 39:10). Lay to heart the advice of wise Solomon: do not merely refuse "to enter the path of the wicked," but "avoid it, do not travel on it, turn away from it, and pass on" (Pro. 4:15). Do not merely avoid drunkenness, but refuse even to "*look* upon the wine when it is red" (Pro. 23:31). The man who took the vow of a Nazarite in Israel, not only took no wine, but he even abstained from grapes in any form whatever. "*Abhor* what is evil," says Paul to the Romans (Romans 12:9); not simply do not do it. "*Flee* youthful lusts," he writes to Timothy; that is, get away from them as far as possible (2 Tim. 2:22). Oh, how necessary are such cautions! Dinah must go out among the wicked Shechemites to see their ways, and as a result she lost her character (Gen. 34). Lot must pitch his tent near sinful Sodom, and he lost everything but his life (see Gen. 13:10-13; 19:1f.).

Young man, be wise in time. Do not be always trying to see how near you can allow the enemy of your soul to come, and yet escape him. Hold him at arm's length. Try to keep clear of temptation as far as possible, and this will be one great help to keep clear of sin.

**(3) For another thing, resolve never to forget the eye of God.** The eye of God! Think of that. Everywhere, in every house, in every field, in every room, in every company, alone or in a crowd, the eye of God is always upon you. "The eyes of the Lord are in every place, beholding the evil and the good" (Pro. 15:3), and they are eyes that read hearts as well as actions (Heb. 4:12,13).

Endeavor, I beseech you, to realize this fact. Remember that you have to deal with an all-seeing God, - a God who never slumbers nor sleeps (Ps. 121:4), - a God who understands your thoughts afar off (Ps. 139:2), and with whom the night shines as the day. You may leave your father's house, and go away, like the prodigal, into a far country, and think that there is nobody to watch your conduct; but the eye and ear of God are there before you. You may deceive your parents or employers, you may tell them falsehoods, and be one thing before their faces, and another behind their backs, but you cannot deceive God. He knows you through and through. He heard what you said as you spoke to people today. He knows what you are thinking of at this minute. He has set your most secret sins in the light of His countenance, and they will one day come out before the world to your shame, unless you take heed.

How little is this really felt! How many things are done continually, which men would never do if they thought they were seen! How many matters are transacted in the chambers of imagination, which would never bear the light of day! Yes; men entertain thoughts in private, and say words in private, and do acts in private, which they would be ashamed and blush to have exposed before the world. The sound of a footstep coming has stopped many a deed of wickedness. A knock at the door has caused many an evil work to be hastily suspended, and hurriedly laid aside. But oh, what miserable driveling folly is all this! There is an all-seeing Witness with us wherever we go. Lock the door, draw down the blinds, close the shutters, put out the light; it does not matter, it makes no difference; God is everywhere, you cannot shut Him out, or prevent His seeing. "All things are naked and open to the eyes of Him to whom we must give account" (Heb. 4:13). Well did young Joseph understand this when his master's wife tempted him. There was no one in the house to see them, no human eye to witness against him; but Joseph was one who lived as seeing Him that is invisible: "How can I do this great wickedness," he said, "and sin against God?" (Gen. 39:9).

Young man, I ask you to read Psalm 139. I advise you to learn it by heart.[36] Make it the test of all your dealings in this world's business: say to yourself often, "Do I remember that God sees me?"

Live as in the sight of God. This is what Abraham did, - he walked *before* Him. This is what Enoch did, - he walked *with* Him. This is what heaven itself will be, - the eternal presence of God. *Do* nothing you would not like God to see. *Say* nothing you would not like God to hear. *Write* nothing you would not like God to read. *Go* to no place where you would not like God to find you. *Read* no book of which you would not like God to say, "Show it to Me." Never spend your time in such a way that you would not like to have God say, "What are you doing?"

**(4) For another thing, be diligent in the use of all public means of grace.** Be regular in going to the house of God, whenever it is open for prayer and preaching, and it is in your power to attend. Be regular in keeping the Lord's Day holy, and determine that God's Day out of the seven shall hereafter always be given to its rightful owner.

I would not leave any false impression on your minds. Do not go away and say that I told you that keeping your church duties made up the whole of true religion. I tell you no such thing. I have no wish to see you grow up formalists and Pharisees. If you think the mere carrying of your body to a certain house, at certain times, on a certain day in the week, will make you a Christian, and prepare you to meet God, I tell you flatly you are miserably deceived. All services without heart service are unprofitable and vain. They only are true worshippers who "worship God in spirit and in truth: the Father seeks such to worship Him" (John 4:23).

But means of grace are not to be despised because they are not saviors. Gold is not food, - you cannot eat it, - but you would not therefore say it is useless, and throw it away. Your soul's eternal well-being most certainly does not depend on means of grace, but it is no less certain that without them, as a general rule, your soul will not be well. God *might* take all who are saved to heaven in a chariot of fire, as He did Elijah, but He does not do so. He *might* teach them all by visions, and dreams, and miraculous interventions, without requiring them to read or think for themselves, but He does not do so. And why not? Because He is a God that works by means, and it is His law and will that in all man's dealings with Him means shall be used. None but a fool or fanatic would think of building a house without ladders and scaffolding, and just so no wise man will despise means, especially when ordained by God.

I dwell more on this point, because Satan will try hard to fill your minds with arguments against the use of means. He will draw your attention to the numbers of persons who use them and are no better for the using. "See there," he will whisper, "do you not observe that those who go to church are no better than those who stay away?"[37] But do not let this move you. It is never fair to argue against a thing because it is improperly used. It does not follow that means of grace can do no good because many attend on them and get no good from them. Medicine is not to be despised because many take it and do not recover their health. No man would think of giving up eating and drinking because others choose to eat and drink improperly, and so make themselves ill. The value of the means of grace, like other things, depends, in a great measure, on the manner and spirit in which we use them.

I dwell on this point too, because of the strong anxiety I feel that every young man should regularly hear the preaching of Christ's gospel. I cannot tell you how important I think this is. By God's blessing, the ministry of the gospel might be the means of converting your soul, - of leading you to a saving knowledge of Christ, - of making you a child of God in deed and in truth. This would be cause for eternal thankfulness indeed. This would be an event over which angels would rejoice. But even if this were not the case, there is a *restraining* power and influence in the ministry of the gospel, under which I earnestly desire every young man to be brought. There are thousands whom it keeps back from evil, though it has not yet turned them unto God; it has made them far better members of society, though it has not yet made them true Christians. There is a certain kind of mysterious power in the faithful preaching of the gospel, which insensibly affects multitudes who listen to it without receiving it into their hearts. To hear sin cried down, and holiness cried up, to hear Christ exalted, and the works of the devil denounced, - to hear the kingdom of heaven and its blessedness described, and the world and its emptiness exposed; to hear this week after week, Sunday after Sunday, is seldom without good effect to the soul. It makes it far harder afterwards to run into any excessive and riotous living. It acts as a wholesome check upon a man's heart. This, I believe, is one way in which that promise of God is made good, "My Word shall not return unto Me void" - (Isa. 55:11). There is much truth in that strong saying of Whitefield,[38] "The gospel keeps many a one from the jail and gallows, even if it does not keep him from hell."

Let me here name another point which is closely connected with this subject. Let nothing ever tempt you to become a Sabbath-breaker.[39] I press this on your attention. Make conscience of giving all your Sabbath to God. A spirit of disregard for this holy day is growing up among us with fearful rapidity, and not least among young men. Sunday traveling, Sunday visiting, Sunday outings, are becoming every year more common than they were, and are doing infinite harm to souls.[40]

Young man, be jealous on this point. Whether you live in town or country, take a decided stand, and resolve not to profane your Sabbath. Let not the plausible argument of "needful relaxation for your body," let not the example of all around you, let not the invitation of companions with whom you may be thrown; let none of these things move you to depart from this settled rule, that *God's Day shall be given to God.*

Once you give up caring for the Sabbath, in the end you will give up caring for your soul. The steps which lead to this conclusion are easy and regular. Begin with not honoring God's Day, and you will soon not honor God's House; - cease to honor God's House, and you will soon cease to honor God's Book; cease to honor God's Book, and ultimately you will give God no honor at all. Let a man lay the foundation of having *no Sabbath*, and I am never surprised if he finishes with the top-stone of *no God*. It is a remarkable saying of Judge Hale, "Of all the persons who were convicted of capital crimes while he was upon the bench, he found only a few who would not confess, on inquiry, that they began their career of wickedness by a neglect of the Sabbath."[41]

Young man, you may be thrown among companions who forget the honor of the Lord's Day; but resolve, by God's help, that you will always remember to keep it holy. Honor it by a regular attendance at some place where the gospel is preached. Settle down under a faithful ministry, and once settled, let your place in church never be empty. Believe me, you will find a special blessing following you: "If you call the Sabbath a delight, the holy day of the Lord honorable; and shall honor Him, not doing your own ways, nor finding your own pleasure, nor speaking your own words: then you shall delight yourself in the Lord; and I will cause you to ride on the high hills of the earth" (Isa. 58:13, 14). And one thing is very certain, your feelings about the Sabbath will always be a test and gauge of your fitness for heaven. They are a fore- taste and fragment of heaven. The man who finds them a burden and not a privilege may be sure that his heart stands in need of a mighty change.

**(5) And one last thing, resolve that wherever you are, you will pray.** Prayer is the life-breath of a man's soul. Without it, we may have a name to live, and be counted Christians; but we are dead in the sight of God. The feeling that we must cry to God for mercy and peace is a mark of grace; and the habit of spreading before Him our soul's needs is an evidence that we have the spirit of adoption. And prayer is the appointed way to obtain the relief of our spiritual necessities. It opens the treasury, and sets the fountain flowing. If we have not, it is because we ask not (Jas. 4:3).

Prayer is the way to procure the outpouring of the Spirit upon our hearts. Jesus has promised the Holy Spirit, the Comforter (Jn. 14:16). He is ready to come down with all His precious gifts, renewing, sanctifying, purifying, strengthening, cheering, encouraging, enlightening, teaching, directing and guiding into all truth. But then He waits to be entreated.

And here it is, I say it with sorrow, here it is that men fall short so miserably. Few indeed are to be found who pray: many who go down on their knees, and say a form perhaps, but few who pray; few who cry unto God, few who call upon the Lord, few who seek as if they wanted to find, few who knock as if they hungered and thirsted, few who wrestle, few who strive with God earnestly for an answer, few who give Him no rest, few who continue in prayer, few who watch unto prayer, few who pray always without ceasing, and faint not. Yes: few pray! It is just one of the things assumed as a matter of policy, but seldom practiced; a thing which is everybody's business, but in fact hardly anybody performs.

Young man, believe me, if your soul is to be saved, you must pray. God has no silent children. If you are to resist the world, the flesh, and the devil, you must pray: it is in vain to look for strength in the hour of trial, if it has not been sought for. You may be thrown together with those who never do it, you may have to sleep in the same room with someone who never asks anything of God, - still, mark my words, you must pray.

I can quite believe you find great difficulties about it, difficulties about opportunities, and seasons, and places. I dare not lay down too precise a set of rules on such points as these. I leave them to your own conscience. You must be guided by circumstances. Our Lord Jesus Christ prayed on a mountain; Isaac prayed in the fields; Hezekiah turned his face to the wall as he lay upon his bed; Daniel prayed by the riverside; Peter, the Apostle, on the housetop. I have heard of young men praying in stables and hay-lofts. All that I contend for is this, - you must know what it is to "enter into your closet" (Matt. 6:6). There must be stated times when you must speak to God face to face, you must every day have your seasons for prayer. *You must pray*.

Without this all other advice and counsel is useless. This is that piece of spiritual armor which Paul names last in his list, in Ephesians 6, but it is in truth first in value and importance.[42] This is that meat which you must daily eat, if you would travel safely through the wilderness of this life. It is only in the strength of this that you will get onward towards the mount of God. I have heard it said that the needle-grinders of Sheffield sometimes wear a magnetic mouthpiece at their work, which catches all the fine dust that flies around them, prevents it entering their lungs, and so saves their lives. Prayer is the mouth-piece that you must wear continually, or else you will never work on uninjured by the unhealthy atmosphere of this sinful world. - You must pray.

Young man, be sure no time is so well spent as that which a man spends upon his knees. Make time for this, whatever your employment may be. Think of David, king of Israel: what does he say? "Evening, and morning, and at noon will I pray and cry aloud, and He shall hear my voice" (Ps. 55:17). Think of Daniel. He had all the business of a kingdom on his hands; yet he prayed three times a day (Dan. 6:10).

See there the secret of his safety in wicked Babylon. Think of Solomon. He begins his reign with prayer for help and assistance, and thus his wonderful prosperity (2 Chron. 1:7-12). Think of Nehemiah. He could find time to pray to the God of heaven, even when standing in the presence of his master, Artaxerxes (Neh. 2:4). Think of the example these godly men have left you, and go and do likewise.

Oh that the Lord may give you the Spirit of grace and supplication (Zech. 12:10)! "Will you not from this time cry to Me, 'My Father, You are the guide of my youth?' " (Jer. 3:4). I would gladly allow all the words of this book to be forgotten, if only this doctrine of the importance of prayer were impressed upon your heart.

# 5

## *Concluding Remarks to Young Men*

And now I hasten towards a conclusion. I have said things that many perhaps will not like, and not receive; but I appeal to your conscience, *Are they not true*?

Young man, you *do* have a conscience. Corrupt and ruined by the fall as we are, each of us has a conscience. In a corner of each heart there sits a witness for God, a witness who condemns when we do wrong, and approves when we do right. To that witness I make my appeal this day, *Are not the things that I have been saying true*?

Go then, young man, and resolve this day to remember your Creator in the days of your youth. Before the day of grace is past, before your conscience has become hardened by age, and deadened by repeated trampling under foot, while you have strength, and time, and opportunities, go and join

yourself to the Lord in an everlasting covenant not
to be forgotten (Isa. 55:1-3). The Spirit will not always strive with you. The voice of conscience will
become feebler and fainter every year you continue
to resist it. The Athenians said to Paul, "We will
hear you again on this matter," but they had heard
him for the last time (Acts 17:32). Make haste, and
do not delay. Linger and hesitate no more.

Think of the unspeakable *comfort you will give
to parents*, relatives and friends, if you take my counsel. They have expended time, money, and health to
raise you, and make you what you are. Surely they
deserve some consideration at your hands. Who can
estimate the joy and gladness which young people
have it in their power to occasion? Who can tell the
anxiety and sorrow that sons like Esau, and Hophni,
and Phinehas, and Absalom may cause? Truly indeed does Solomon say, "A wise son makes a glad
father, but a foolish son is the grief of his mother"
(Pro. 10:1). Oh, consider these things, and give God
your heart! Let it not be said of you at last, as it is of
so many, that your "Youth was a blunder, your man-
hood a struggle, and your old age a regret."

Think of the *instruments of good you may be to
the world*. Almost all the most notable saints of God
sought the Lord early. Moses, Samuel, David and
Daniel, all served God from their youth. God seems

to delight in putting special honor upon young servants. And what might we not confidently expect, if young men in our own day would consecrate the springtime of their lives to God? Agents are needed now in almost every great and good cause, and cannot be found. Machinery of every kind for spreading truth exists, but there are not enough hands to work it. Money is more easily gotten for doing good than men. Ministers are needed for new churches, missionaries are needed for new fields, visitors are needed for neglected districts, and teachers are needed for new schools. Many a good cause is standing still merely for lack of agents. The supply of godly, faithful, trustworthy men, for posts like those I have named, is far below the demand.[43]

Young man, in this present day, *you are needed for God.* This is peculiarly an age of activity. We are shaking off some of our past selfishness. Men no longer sleep the sleep of apathy and indifference about others, as their forefathers did. They are beginning to be ashamed of thinking, like Cain, "Am I my brother's keeper?" (Gen. 4:9). A wide field of usefulness is open before you, if you are only willing to enter upon it. The harvest is great, and the laborers are few. Be zealous of good works. Come, come to the help of the Lord's cause against the mighty forces of evil mounting everyday.

This is, in some sort, to be like God, not only "good, but doing good" (Ps. 119:68). This is the way to follow the steps of your Lord and Savior: "He went about doing good". This is to live as David did; he "served his own generation by the will of God" (Acts 13:36).

And who can doubt that this is the path which is most fitting to a never-dying soul? Who would not rather leave this world like Josiah, lamented by all (2 Chron. 35:24,25), than to depart like Jehoram, "to no one's sorrow"? (2 Chron. 21:20). Consider, is it better to be an idle, frivolous, useless cumberer of the ground, to live for your body, your selfishness, your lusts, and your pride, or to spend and be spent in the glorious cause of usefulness to your fellowmen? Is it better to be self-centered, or to be like William Wilberforce[44] or Lord Shaftesbury,[45] a blessing to your country and the world; or to be like Howard,[46] the friend of the prisoner and the captive, to be like Schwartz,[47] the spiritual father of hundreds of never-dying souls in heathen lands, to be like that man of God, Robert Murray M'Cheyne,[48] a burning and a shining light, an epistle of Christ, known and read by all men, the quickener of every Christian heart that comes across your path? Oh, who can doubt? Who can for one moment doubt?

Young man, consider your responsibilities. Think of the privilege and luxury of doing good. Resolve *this day* to be useful. *At once* give your heart to Christ.

Think, finally, of the *happiness that will come to your own soul* if you serve God, happiness by the way, as you travel through life, and happiness in the end, when the journey is over. Believe me, whatever vain notions you may have heard, believe me, there is a reward for the righteous even in *this* world (Luke 18:29,30). Godliness has indeed the promise of this life, as well as of that which is to come (1 Tim. 4:8). There is a solid peace in feeling and knowing that God is your friend. There is a genuine satisfaction in knowing that however great your unworthiness, you are complete in Christ, that you have an enduring portion, that you have chosen that good part which shall not be taken from you (Luke 10:42).

The backslider in heart may well be filled with his own ways, but "a good man shall be satisfied from himself" (Pro. 14:14). The path of the worldly man grows darker and darker every year that he lives; the path of the Christian is as a shining light, brighter and brighter to the very end (Pro. 4:18,19). His sun is just rising when the sun of the worldly is setting forever; his best things are all beginning to blossom and bloom forever, when those of the worldly are all slipping out of his hands, and passing away.

Young man, these things are true. Bear with this word of exhortation. Be persuaded. Take up the cross. Follow Christ. Yield yourself to God.

# End Notes

## Chapter 1

[1] The means of grace, according to the shorter catechism, are the ordinances of God, especially the Word, sacraments and prayer. For an excellent edition of the Baptist Catechism see *The Shorter Catechism: A Baptist Version* recently published in a sturdy paperback by Simpson Publishing Co., P.O. Box 100, Avinger, TX 75630.

[2] Although the precise statistics have no doubt changed in the last 100 years, the fact remains that multitudes of young men and women are ushered into eternity every year.

[3] Jerome (345-420 A.D.) was a Bible translator and advocate of monasticism. His most famous accomplishment was the translation of the Bible into Latin. This translation is known as the Latin Vulgate. By the eighth century this translation became the officially recognized and authorized version of the Bible for the Catholic church, replacing all other Latin translations.

[4] Robert Leighton (1611-1684) was a graduate of Edinburgh University, and Archbishop of Glasgow. Among his devotional writings is a notable commentary on 1 Peter, which C.H. Spurgeon commended by saying, "It is a favorite with all spiritual men."

⁵ This was the lower of the two millstones used for grinding grain. This was often used to describe a condition of hard-heartedness.

⁶ Theodore Beza (1519-1605) was an admirer, friend, associate and successor of John Calvin at Geneva. Although trained to be a lawyer, an illness turned his thoughts to God and to the Reformed Faith.

⁷ See the booklet entitled *A Dying Man's Regrets*, by Adolphe Monod (Calvary Press, 1992) which seeks to deal with many of the issues one regrets upon his death bed. In this little booklet one of the foremost preachers in France last century opens his heart from his death bed to share his personal regrets.

⁸ An excellent series of books has been produced which address these areas in a very simple, yet powerful way. Send for a catalog to Triangle Press, 23 - 5th Ave. S.E., Conrad, MT 59425.

## *Chapter 2*

⁹ Sir Isaac Newton (1642-1727) was a gifted philosopher and mathematician.

¹⁰ Augustine (354-430 A.D.) was the famous Bishop of Hippo. See this account of his famous conversion to Christ in the classic *Confessions*, Book Eight, Chapter XII.

¹¹ Francis Bacon (1561-1626) was an English statesman and philosopher.

[12] Matthew Henry (1662-1714) was a biblical expositor who penned one of the most helpful commentaries on the entire Bible. Several editions of this work are now available. If you desire to know God's Word, purchase a set and read it.

[13] A tragic indication of the modern world's attitude toward this notion is found in the motto of the International Humor Institute: "Not a shred of evidence exists that life is serious."

[14] The word is used here as a synonym of *gullible*.

[15] Is this not the case with regard to creation and evolution? Scripture declares without equivocation that God created the world by His own powerful word. The Lord has turned the so-called wisdom of the world into foolishness (see 1 Cor. 3:18-20), therefore it is ready to argue that this gloriously complex universe happened by mere chance. If you are interested in examining this issue more carefully, write for information to: The Institute of Creation Research at P.O. Box 2667, El Cajon, CA 92021.

[16] John W. Rochester (1647-1680) was an English courtier.

[17] Robert South (1634-1716) was an Anglican clergyman whose sermons have been called "classics of English Divinity." He sought to preach always with clarity, simplicity and fervor.

[18] See the following texts of Scripture which utilize this identical language: Deut. 31:6,7,23; Josh. 1:6,9,18; 10:25; Psalm 27:14.

[19] Col. James Gardiner (1687-1745) was a godly preacher who was remarkably converted while reading Thomas Watson's book, *Heaven Taken by Storm*, which has been recently reprinted by Soli Deo Gloria Publications. For a catalog write them at 213 W. Vincent St., Ligonier, PA 15658.

## *Chapter 3*

[20] There is no better way of becoming acquainted with the Lord Jesus Christ than by reading the Gospels again and again. No better tool exists for understanding the spirit of the Gospels than *Expository Thoughts on the Gospels* by J.C. Ryle. These are presently available in several different editions. They are superb!

[21] The Westminster Assembly's Larger Catechism begins with the admirable question and answer: "What is the chief and highest end of man?" "To glorify God, and fully to enjoy Him forever."

[22] Zeuxis (B.C. 464-396) was a Greek painter.

[23] Augustine spoke these wise words in his classic work- *The Confessions*: "Grant me what Thou commandest, and command what Thou wilt" (Book 10, Chapter XXIX).

²⁴ To examine each of these lives, note the following Scriptures with each man: Isaac (Gen. 22); Joseph (Gen. 39); Joshua (Exodus 17:9-14; 24:13; 33:11); Samuel (1 Sam. 2:18 - 3:21); David (1 Sam. 16,17); Solomon (1 Kings 3:4-9); Obadiah (1 Kings 18:3f.); Josiah (2 Chron. 34,35); and Timothy (Acts 16:1-3). Such biographical study would be of great profit to your soul! For assistance in this study you are encouraged to get a copy of *Letters to Young Men* by William Sprague, reprinted recently by Sprinkle Publications, P.O. Box 1094, Harrisonburg, VA 22801. He examines the life of Joseph.

²⁵ John Bunyan's (1628-1688) classic *Pilgrim's Progress* is a book worthy of your careful and prayerful examination. It is not possible to exaggerate the value of this book. If you do not have a copy, get one and read it. Spurgeon read it over 100 times.

²⁶ Charles Bridges has a very helpful commentary on the entire 119th Psalm which is available from the Banner of Truth Trust. The godly Matthew Henry taught his children that the best way to fall in love with the Bible was daily to meditate upon Psalm 119.

²⁷ Geoffrey Thomas has written a very helpful little booklet entitled *Reading the Bible*, which is published by The Banner of Truth Trust. This booklet features a daily reading schedule which would enable you to complete the Old Testament once in a year and the New Testament twice. Find some method that works for you and stick with it, no matter what.

[28] William Beveridge (1637-1708) was an Anglican bishop of Asaph, England.

[29] Tragically our age is *not* an age of reading. Young man, be determined to resist this tragic tendency, and read, read, read!

## *Chapter 4*

[30] A midge is a very tiny fly, abundant in parts of the United States and Canada.

[31] William Bridge (1600-1670) was a pastor and writer whose works have been recently reprinted by Soli Deo Gloria Publications.

[32] Juvenal (34-120) was a Roman satirical poet.

[33] Jeremy Taylor (1613-1667) was an Anglican bishop and writer who was born and educated at Cambridge. He wrote a few very helpful books including, *Holy Living* and *Holy Dying.*

[34] Joseph Hall (1574-1656) was the Bishop of Norwich. His book *Hard Times* relates his poverty and suffering at the hands of Parliament.

[35] There is an old fable, that the butterfly once asked the owl how she should deal with the fire which had singed her wings; and the owl counseled her, in reply, not to consider even as much as its smoke.

[36] The godly Puritan Samuel Annesley (1620-1696) said the following about Psalm 139: "This is one psalm which it were well if Christians would repeat every morning and evening." Also Matthew Poole (1624-1679) said the following, "This psalm is esteemed by the Hebrews the most excellent in the whole book. The matter of it is noble and sublime."

[37] C.S. Lewis (1898-1963) was an Anglican layman who taught at both Oxford and Cambridge. In his famous book *The Screwtape Letters* the devil uses very similar arguments to seek to dissuade a new convert from his faith (see chapter 2).

[38] George Whitefield (1714-1770) was one of the greatest evangelists in Church History. Arnold Dallimore has given us the definitive biography of this man published in two volumes by *Cornerstone Books*, 9825 W. Roosevelt, Westchester, IL 60153.

[39] For a recent treatment of the Sabbath issue see the book *Call the Sabbath a Delight*, by Walter Chantry published by the Banner of Truth Trust.

[40] It is obvious from Ryle's language that the observance of the Sabbath in his day was far stricter than is generally true in our day. Let the thoughtful reader consider if our laxness displays an evidence of advance or decline in true piety.

[41] Sir Matthew Hale (1609-1676) was a famous English jurist and writer. Capital crimes were those punishable by death.

[42] See the words of George Duffield's famous hymn:

> *"Stand up, stand up for Jesus,*
> *stand in His strength alone;*
> *the arm of flesh will fail you,*
> *ye dare not trust your own:*
> *put on the gospel armor,*
> **each piece put on with prayer.**
> *where duty calls, or danger,*
> *be never wanting there."*

## Chapter 5

[43] For an outstanding tool to make you aware of the great needs and opportunities for the gospel in our day, purchase a copy of *Operation World*, by Patrick Johnstone. This book is published by Send the Light Books, at PO Box 28, Waynesboro, GA 30830, USA. It is set up in the form of a daily prayer guide which can be used to awaken you to the needs and opportunities which exist throughout the world. Soon to be published is a children's version by his wife Jill.

[44] William Wilberforce (1759-1833) was an English statesman, philanthropist and abolitionist. He labored to abolish the trafficking of slaves and the institution of slavery. He died one month before the

Emancipation Bill passed officially ending the slave trade in all the British Colonies.

[45] Anthony A. Shaftesbury (1801-1885) was a man of God, committed to reforming many inhumane practices in England.

[46] John Howard (1726-1790) was an English philanthropist and advocate of prison reform who spent his life seeking to expose and improve the horribly inhumane conditions of prisons.

[47] Christian F. Schwartz (1726-1798) was a German missionary to India whose labors over 40 years were blessed by God in establishing schools and congregations throughout southern India.

[48] M'Cheyne (1813-1843) was one of the most godly men of the last century. I urge you to acquire a copy of Andrew Bonar's <u>Memoir and Remains of Robert Murray M'Cheyne</u>, published by *The Banner of Truth Trust*.

# NOTES

# NOTES

# NOTES_____

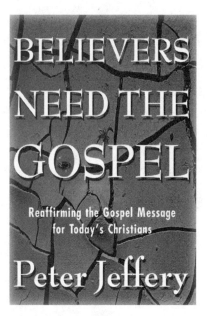

*Believers Need The Gospel*

They were captivated by its message. They settled into their new lives and began to learn the need for holiness and discipleship, but imperceptibly, perhaps, there grew in them a tendency to lose the simple thrill of being saved. Peter Jeffery reawakens us to the power of God found in the foundational message of our lives. (**Softcover**)

1-800-789-8175 / www.calvarypress.com

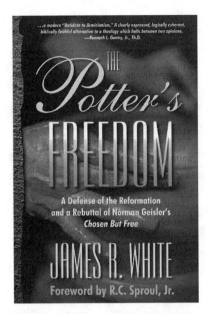

*...a modern "Antidote to Arminianism." A clearly expressed, logically coherent, biblically faithful alternative to a theology which halts between two opinions.*
—Kenneth L. Gentry, Jr., Th.D.

THE *Potter's* FREEDOM

A Defense of the Reformation and a Rebuttal of Norman Geisler's *Chosen But Free*

JAMES R. WHITE

Foreword by R.C. Sproul, Jr.

### *The Potter's Freedom*

This landmark book by James White was written as a reply to Dr. Norman Geisler's recent attack on the doctrines of grace, but it is much more—it is a defense of the Protestant Reformation and the very gospel itself! "Firmly, pointedly, and charitably written," writes **Douglas Wilson.** Foreword by **R.C. Sproul, Jr. (Large Softcover)**

# CALVARY PRESS
# OUR MISSION

The ministry of Calvary Press is firmly committed to printing quality Christian literature relevant to the dire needs of the church and the world at the dawn of the 21st century. We unashamedly stand upon the foundation stones of the Reformation of the 16th century—Scripture alone, Faith alone, Grace alone, Christ alone, and God's Glory alone!

Our prayer for this ministry is found in two portions taken from the Psalms: "And let the beauty of the LORD our God be upon us, And establish the work of our hands for us; Yes, establish the work of our hands," and "Not unto us, O LORD, not unto us, but to Your name give glory" (Ps. 90:17; 115:1).

For a FREE catalog of all our titles,
please be sure to call us at:
**1-800-789-8175**
or visit our online store:
www.calvarypress.com